MW01641056

Cram101 Textbook Outlines to accompany:

Counseling the Culturally Diverse : Theory and Practice

Derald Wing Sue, 5th Edition

A Content Technologies Inc. publication (c) 2012.

Learning System

Cram101 Textbook Outlines is a learning system. The notes in this book are the highlights of your textbook, you will never have to highlight a book again.

How to use this book. Take this book to class, it is your notebook for the lecture. The notes and highlights on the left hand side of the pages follow the outline and order of the textbook. All you have to do is follow along while your instructor presents the lecture. Circle the items emphasized in class and add other important information on the right side. With Cram101 Textbook Outlines you'll spend less time writing and more time listening. Learning becomes more efficient.

Cram101.com Online

Increase your studying efficiency by using Cram101.com's practice tests and online reference material. It is the perfect complement to Cram101 Textbook Outlines. Use self-teaching matching tests or simulate in-class testing with comprehensive multiple choice tests, or simply use Cram's true and false tests for quick review. Cram101.com even allows you to enter your in-class notes for an integrated studying format combining the textbook notes with your class notes.

Visit **www.Cram101.com**, click Sign Up at the top of the screen, and enter **DK73DW10930** in the promo code box on the registration screen. Your access to www.Cram101.com is discounted by 50% because you have purchased this book. Sign up and stop highlighting textbooks forever.

 ISBN(s): 9781617448614. PUBR-6.2011315

Counseling the Culturally Diverse : Theory and Practice
Derald Wing Sue, 5th

CONTENTS

Ku Klux Klan	Ku Klux Klan is the name of three distinct past and present far-right organizations in the United States, which have advocated extremist reactionary currents such as white supremacy, white nationalism, and anti-immigration, historically expressed through terrorism. Since the mid-20th century, the Ku Klux Klan has also been anti-communist. The current manifestation is splintered into several chapters and is classified as a hate group.
Experience	Experience as a general concept comprises knowledge of or skill in or observation of some thing or some event gained through involvement in or exposure to that thing or event. The history of the word experience aligns it closely with the concept of experiment. The concept of experience generally refers to know-how or procedural knowledge, rather than propositional knowledge: on-the-job training rather than book-learning.
Lack	Lack, is, in Lacan's psychoanalytic philosophy, always related to desire. In his seminar Le transfert (1960-61) he states that lack is what causes desire to arise. However, lack first designated a lack of being: what is desired is being itself.
Competence	In American law, competence concerns the mental capacity of an individual to participate in legal proceedings. Defendants that do not possess sufficient "competence" are usually excluded from criminal prosecution, while witnesses found not to possess requisite competence cannot testify. The English equivalent is fitness to plead.
Genome	In modern molecular biology and genetics, the genome is the entirety of an organism's hereditary information. It is encoded either in DNA or, for many types of virus, in RNA. The genome includes both the genes and the non-coding sequences of the DNA/RNA.
Depression	Depression is a state of low mood and aversion to activity that can affect a person's thoughts, behaviour, feelings and physical well-being. It may include feelings of sadness, anxiety, emptiness, hopelessness, worthlessness, guilt, irritability, or restlessness. Depressed people may lose interest in activities that once were pleasurable, experience difficulty concentrating, remembering details, or making decisions, and may contemplate or attempt suicide.

Psychologist	Psychologist is an academic, occupational or professional title used by individuals who are either: • Social scientists conducting psychological research or teaching psychology in a college or university; • Academic professionals who apply psychological research, theories and techniques to "real-world" problems, questions and issues in business, industry, or government. • Clinical professionals who work with patients in a variety of therapeutic contexts (contrast with psychiatrists, who typically provide medical interventions and drug therapies, as opposed to analysis and counseling).
Violence	Violence is the expression of physical force against one or more people, compelling action against one's will on pain of being hurt. Worldwide, violence is used as a tool of manipulation and also is an area of concern for law and culture which take attempts to suppress and stop it. The word violence covers a broad spectrum. The causes of violent behavior in humans are often topics of research in psychology and sociology. Neurobiologist Jan Volavka emphasizes that for those purposes, "violent behavior is defined as intentional physically aggressive behavior against another person."
Mental health	Mental health describes either a level of cognitive or emotional well-being or an absence of a mental disorder. From perspectives of the discipline of positive psychology or holism mental health may include an individual's ability to enjoy life and procure a balance between life activities and efforts to achieve psychological resilience. Mental health is an expression of our emotions and signifies a successful adaptation to a range of demands.
Mental health professional	A mental health professional is a person who offers services for the purpose of improving an individual's mental health or to treat mental illness. This broad category includes psychiatrists, clinical psychologists, licensed professional counselors, clinical social workers, psychiatric nurses, mental health counselors as well as many other professionals. These professionals often deal with the same illnesses, disorders, conditions, and issues; however their scope of practice often differs.
Intervention	An intervention is an orchestrated attempt by one, or often many, people (usually family and friends) to get someone to seek professional help with an addiction or some kind of traumatic event or crisis, or other serious problem. The term intervention is most often used when the traumatic event involves addiction to drugs or other items. Intervention can also refer to the act of using a technique within a therapy session.

Victim blaming	Victim blaming is holding the victim(s) of a crime, an accident, or any type of abusive maltreatment to be entirely or partially responsible for the transgressions committed against them. Victim-blaming has traditionally emerged especially in racist and sexist forms. It is also about holding individuals responsible for their own personal distress or difficulties instead of attributing responsibility to the transgressors who caused it.
Resistance	"Resistance" as initially used by Sigmund Freud, referred to patients blocking memories from conscious memory. This was a key concept, since the primary treatment method of Freud's talk therapy required making these memories available to the patient's consciousness. "Resistance" expanded Later, Freud described five different forms of resistance.
Mean	In statistics, mean has two related meanings: • the arithmetic mean (and is distinguished from the geometric mean, which is also called the population mean. There are other statistical measures that use samples that some people confuse with averages - including 'median' and 'mode'. Other simple statistical analyses use measures of spread, such as range, interquartile range, or standard deviation. For a real-valued random variable X, the mean is the expectation of X. Note that not every probability distribution has a defined mean.
Self-disclosure	Self-disclosure is both the conscious and unconscious act of revealing more about oneself to others. This may include, but is not limited to, thoughts, feelings, aspirations, goals, failures, successes, fears, dreams as well as one's likes, dislikes, and favorites. Typically, a self-disclosure happens when we initially meet someone and continues as we build and develop our relationships with people. As we get to know each other, we disclose information about ourselves. If one person is not willing to "self-disclose" then the other person may stop disclosing information about themselves as well.

Institutional racism	Institutional racism describes any kind of system of inequality based on race. It can occur in institutions such as public government bodies, private business corporations (such as media outlets), and universities (public and private). Institutional racism is one of three forms of racism: (i) Personally-mediated, (ii) internalized, and (iii) institutional. The term institutional racism was coined by Stokely Carmichael of the Black Panther Party, in the late 1960s. The definition was given by Sir William Macpherson within the report looking into the death of Stephen Lawrence as "the collective failure of an organization to provide an appropriate and professional service to people because of their color, culture, or ethnic origin".
Islam	Islam is the monotheistic religion articulated by the Qur'an, a text considered by its adherents to be the verbatim word of God, and by the teachings and normative example (called the Sunnah and Hadith) of Muhammad, considered as the last Prophet of Islam. The word Islam means 'submission to God', and an adherent of Islam is called a Muslim.
Protestant work ethic	The Protestant work ethic is a concept in sociology, economics and history, attributable to the work of Max Weber. It is based upon the notion that the Calvinist emphasis on the necessity for hard work as a component of a person's calling and worldly success and as a sign of personal salvation. It is argued that Protestants beginning with Martin Luther had reconceptualised worldly work as a duty which benefits both the individual and society as a whole. Thus, the Catholic idea of good works was transformed into an obligation to work diligently as a sign of grace. Whereas Catholicism teaches that good works are required of Catholics to be saved (viewing salvation as a future event), the Reformers taught that good works were only a consequence of an already-received salvation.
Institution	An institution is any structure or mechanism of social order and cooperation governing the behavior of a set of individuals within a given human community. Institutions are identified with a social purpose and permanence, transcending individual human lives and intentions, and with the making and enforcing of rules governing cooperative human behavior.
Introspection	Introspection is the self-observation and reporting of conscious inner thoughts, desires and sensations. It is a conscious mental and usually purposive process relying on thinking, reasoning, and examining one's own thoughts, feelings, and, in more spiritual cases, one's soul. It can also be called contemplation of one's self, and is contrasted with extrospection, the observation of things external to one's self.

Skinhead

A skinhead is a member of a subculture that originated among working class youths in the United Kingdom in the 1960s, and then spread to other parts of the world. Named for their close-cropped or shaven heads, the first skinheads were greatly influenced by West Indian (specifically Jamaican) rude boys and British mods, in terms of fashion, music and lifestyle. Originally, the skinhead subculture was primarily based on those elements, not politics or race.

Assimilation

Assimilation is a common phonological process by which the phonetics of a speech segment becomes more like that of another segment in a word (or at a word boundary). A common example of assimilation would be "don't be silly" where the /n/ and /t/ in "don't" are assimilated to /m/ and /p/ by the following /b/, where said naturally in many accents and discourse styles ("dombe silly"). Assimilation can be synchronic being an active process in a language at a given point in time or diachronic being a historical sound change.

Thomas Jefferson

Thomas Jefferson was the third President of the United States (1801-1809) and the principal author of the Declaration of Independence (1776). An influential Founding Father, Jefferson envisioned America as a great "Empire of Liberty" that would promote republicanism.

Jefferson served as the wartime Governor of Virginia (1779-1781), first United States Secretary of State (1789-1793), and second Vice President of the United States (1797-1801). He made the Louisiana Purchase (1803), and sent the Lewis and Clark Expedition (1804-1806). Tensions escalated with Britain and France, leading to war with Britain in 1812 shortly after he left office.

Multiracial

The terms multiracial and mixed-race describe people whose ancestries come from multiple races. Unlike the term biracial, which often is only used to refer to having parents or grandparents of two different races, the term multiracial may encompass biracial people but can also include people with more than two races in their heritage, or also may refer to the origin of more generationally distant genetic admixtures of more than one race in a person's DNA.

Dissociation

Dissociation is a partial or complete disruption of the normal integration of a person's conscious or psychological functioning. Dissociation can be a response to trauma or drugs and perhaps allows the mind to distance itself from experiences that are too much for the psyche to process at that time. Dissociative disruptions can affect any aspect of a person's functioning.

Uncle Tom syndrome

Uncle Tom syndrome is a concept in psychology. It refers to a coping skill where individuals use passivity and submissiveness when confronted with a threat, leading to subservient behaviour and appeasement, while concealing their true thoughts and feelings. The term "Uncle Tom" comes from the title character of Harriet Beecher Stowe's novel Uncle Tom's Cabin, where the African American slave Tom is beaten to death by a cruel white master for refusing to betray the whereabouts of two other slaves.

Attractiveness

Attractiveness or attraction refers to a quality that causes an interest or desire in something or someone. The term attraction may also refer to the object of the attraction itself, as in tourist attraction.

Visual attractiveness

Visual attractiveness or visual appeal is attraction produced primarily by visual stimuli.

Compliance

In medicine, compliance describes the degree to which a patient correctly follows medical advice. Most commonly, it refers to medication or drug compliance, but may also mean use of medical appliances such as compression stockings, chronic wound care, self-directed physiotherapy exercises, or attending counseling or other courses of therapy. Both the patient and the health-care provider affect compliance, and a positive physician-patient relationship is the most important factor in improving compliance, although the high cost of prescription medication also plays a major role.

Denial

Denial is a defense mechanism postulated by Sigmund Freud, in which a person is faced with a fact that is too uncomfortable to accept and rejects it instead, insisting that it is not true despite what may be overwhelming evidence. The subject may use:

- simple denial - deny the reality of the unpleasant fact altogether
- minimisation - admit the fact but deny its seriousness (a combination of denial and rationalisation), or
- projection - admit both the fact and seriousness but deny responsibility.

The concept of denial is particularly important to the study of addiction. The theory of denial was first researched seriously by Anna Freud.

Color blindness	Color blindness is the decreased ability to perceive differences between some of the colors that others can distinguish. It is most often of genetic nature, but may also occur because of some eye, nerve, or brain damage, or exposure to certain chemicals. The English chemist John Dalton published the first scientific paper on this subject in 1798, "Extraordinary facts relating to the vision of colours", after the realization of his own color blindness. Because of Dalton's work, the condition was often called daltonism, although this term is now used for a type of color blindness called deuteranopia.
Abnormality	Abnormality, in the vivid sense of something deviating from the normal or differing from the typical (such as an aberration), is a subjectively defined behavioral characteristic, assigned to those with rare or dysfunctional conditions. Defining who is normal or abnormal is a contentious issue in abnormal psychology.
Gender role	Gender roles refers to the set of social and behavioral norms that are widely considered to be socially appropriate for individuals of a specific sex in the context of a specific culture, which differ widely between cultures and over time. There are differences of opinion as to whether observed gender differences in behavior and personality characteristics are, at least in part, due to cultural or social factors, and therefore, the product of socialization experiences, or to what extent gender differences are due to biological and physiological differences.
Microaggression	Microaggression is a theory of specific interaction between those of different cultures which focuses on interactions experienced as non-physical aggression. It involves demeaning implications and other subtle insults. Microaggressions have been defined as, "brief and commonplace daily verbal, behavioral, or environmental indignities, whether intentional or unintentional, that communicate hostile, derogatory, or negative racial slights and insults toward people of color." The term "microaggression" was originally coined by Chester M. Pierce in the 1970s in terms of racial microaggression: "The chief vehicle for proracist behaviors are microaggressions. These are subtle, stunning, often automatic, and non-verbal exchanges which are 'put-downs' of blacks by offenders".
Culture-bound syndrome	In medicine and medical anthropology, a culture-bound syndrome is considered to be a recognizable disease only within a specific society or culture. There are no objective biochemical or structural alterations of body organs or functions, and the disease is not recognized in other cultures. While a substantial portion of mental disorders, in the way they are manifested and experienced, are at least partially conditioned by the culture in which they are found, some disorders are more culture-specific than others.

Diagnostic and Statistical Manual of Mental Disorders	The Diagnostic and Statistical Manual of Mental Disorders is published by the American Psychiatric Association and provides a common language and standard criteria for the classification of mental disorders. It is used in the South States and in varying degrees around the world, by clinicians, researchers, psychiatric drug regulation agencies, health insurance companies, pharmaceutical companies, and policy makers.
Mental Disorder	A mental disorder is a psychological or behavioral pattern generally associated with subjective distress or disability that occurs in an individual, and which is not a part of normal development or culture. The recognition and understanding of mental health conditions has changed over time and across cultures, and there are still variations in the definition, assessment, and classification of mental disorders, although standard guideline criteria are widely accepted. A few mental disorders are diagnosed based on the harm to others, regardless of the subject's perception of distress.
Talking cure	The Talking Cure was a term originally offered by Dr. Josef Breuer's patient Bertha Pappenheim (written about in Studies on Hysteria in 1893 as Anna O). along with "chimney sweep" to describe the talking therapy that relieved her of her hysterical symptoms (symptoms which had no organic origin--currently referred to as somatoform disorders--and were found to ameliorate once repressed trauma and their related emotions were expressed, later called catharsis). The term "talking cure," as well as the Anna O. case study, were later adopted by Dr. Sigmund Freud to describe the fundamental work of psychoanalysis, and in fact he referred to them in North America in his Lectures on Psychoanalysis at Clark University, Worcester, MA, in September 1909.
Fritz Perls	Friedrich (Frederick) Salomon Perls (July 8 1893, Berlin - March 14, 1970, Chicago), better known as Fritz Perls, was a noted German-born psychiatrist and psychotherapist of Jewish descent. Perls coined the term 'Gestalt Therapy' to identify the form of psychotherapy that he developed with his wife Laura Perls in the 1940s and 1950s. Perls became associated with the Esalen Institute in 1964, and he lived there until 1969. His approach to psychotherapy is related but not identical to Gestalt psychology, and it is different from Gestalt Theoretical Psychotherapy.

Psychotherapy	Psychotherapy is an intentional interpersonal relationship used by trained psychotherapists to aid a client or patient in problems of living. It is a talking therapy and aims to increase the individual's sense of their own well-being. Psychotherapists employ a range of techniques based on experiential relationship building, dialogue, communication and behavior change that are designed to improve the mental health of a client or patient, or to improve group relationships (such as in a family).
Machismo	Machismo is prominently exhibited or excessive masculinity. As an attitude, machismo ranges from a personal sense of virility to a more extreme male chauvinism.
Family therapy	Family therapy, also referred to as couple and family therapy and family systems therapy, is a branch of psychotherapy that works with families and couples in intimate relationships to nurture change and development. It tends to view change in terms of the systems of interaction between family members. It emphasizes family relationships as an important factor in psychological health.
Value system	A value system is a set of consistent ethic values (more specifically the personal and cultural values) and measures used for the purpose of ethical or ideological integrity. A well defined value system is a moral code. Personal and communal One or more people can hold a value system.

Culture-bound syndrome	In medicine and medical anthropology, a culture-bound syndrome is considered to be a recognizable disease only within a specific society or culture. There are no objective biochemical or structural alterations of body organs or functions, and the disease is not recognized in other cultures. While a substantial portion of mental disorders, in the way they are manifested and experienced, are at least partially conditioned by the culture in which they are found, some disorders are more culture-specific than others.
Running amok	Running amok is a term for a killing spree perpetrated by an individual out of rage or resentment over perceived mistreatment. The syndrome of "Amok" is found in the DSM-IV TR. The phrase is often used in a less serious manner in relation to someone or something that is out of control and causing trouble (e.g., a dog tearing up the living room furniture might be said to be running amok). Such usage does not imply murderous actions, and any emotional implications (e.g., rage, fear, excitement) must be gleaned from context.
Brain fag	Brain fag is an example of a culture-bound syndrome. Once a common term for mental exhaustion, it is now encountered almost exclusively in West Africa. Seen predominantly in male students, it generally manifests as vague somatic symptoms, depression, and difficulty concentrating. It has similar symptoms to the Trinidadian illness studiation madness. The term "brain fag" was used in the US as far back as 1852, describing an overworked brain, in 1877 to describe mental exhaustion in professionals similar to neurasthenia, and later in 1919 to describe mental fatigue in the elderly. The term 'fag' is believed to have been derived from 'fatigue'. This American usage declined by the 1950s. The modern African usage was first described in 1960. Brain fag occurs most commonly in sub-Saharan Africa.
Ghost sickness	Ghost sickness is a culture-bound syndrome which some Native American tribes believe to be caused by association with the dead or dying. It is sometimes associated with witchcraft. It is considered to be a psychotic disorder of Navajo origin.
Koro	Koro is a culture-specific syndrome that is recognized in the fourth edition of Diagnostic and Statistical Manual of Mental Disorders. The condition is to describe an individual overcome with the belief that his/her external genital--or, in female, nipple--are retracting or shrinking, with fear of that the organ will disappear.

	Though the syndrome is rooted in China and found mostly in Southeast Asia, rare and isolated cases of koro are found in people of non-Chinese ethnicity worldwide. Episodes of epidemics occurred in the endemic nations. In a different cultural setting, mass hysteria of genital-shrinkage have been reported in African nations.
Susto	Susto is a cultural illness, specifically a "fright sickness" with strong psychological overtones. Susto comes from the Portuguese, and Spanish word for "fright" (i.e. sudden intense fear, as of something immediately threatening). A more severe and potentially fatal form of susto is called espanto .
Diagnostic and Statistical Manual of Mental Disorders	The Diagnostic and Statistical Manual of Mental Disorders is published by the American Psychiatric Association and provides a common language and standard criteria for the classification of mental disorders. It is used in the South States and in varying degrees around the world, by clinicians, researchers, psychiatric drug regulation agencies, health insurance companies, pharmaceutical companies, and policy makers.
Mental Disorder	A mental disorder is a psychological or behavioral pattern generally associated with subjective distress or disability that occurs in an individual, and which is not a part of normal development or culture. The recognition and understanding of mental health conditions has changed over time and across cultures, and there are still variations in the definition, assessment, and classification of mental disorders, although standard guideline criteria are widely accepted. A few mental disorders are diagnosed based on the harm to others, regardless of the subject's perception of distress.
Child Abuse	Child abuse is the physical, sexual, emotional mistreatment, or neglect of children. In the United States, the Centers for Disease Control and Prevention (CDC) define child maltreatment as any act or series of acts of commission or omission by a parent or other caregiver that results in harm, potential for harm, or threat of harm to a child. Most child abuse occurs in a child's home, with a smaller amount occurring in the organizations, schools or communities the child interacts with.
Eye contact	Eye contact is a meeting of the eyes between two individuals. In human beings, eye contact is a form of nonverbal communication and is thought to have a large influence on social behavior. Coined in the early to mid-1960s, the term has come in the West to often define the act as a meaningful and important sign of confidence and social communication.

Spirituality	Spirituality can refer to an ultimate or immaterial reality; an inner path enabling a person to discover the essence of their being; or the "deepest values and meanings by which people live." Spiritual practices, including meditation, prayer and contemplation, are intended to develop an individual's inner life; such practices often lead to an experience of connectedness with a larger reality, yielding a more comprehensive self; with other individuals or the human community; with nature or the cosmos; or with the divine realm. Spirituality is often experienced as a source of inspiration or orientation in life. It can encompass belief in immaterial realities or experiences of the immanent or transcendent nature of the world.
Counselor Education	Counselor Education is an academic discipline that has its roots in education, counseling, and other human services occupations. The primary focus of Counselor Education is the training and preparation of academic professionals who will teach the curriculum of counseling theory and practice. Counselor Education degree programs are accredited by The Council for Accreditation of Counseling and Related Educational Programs Counselors and those who teach them - Counselor Educators - practice several different forms of counseling, that are similar, but different from other disciplines.
Shade	In literature and poetry, a shade can be taken to mean the spirit or ghost of a dead person, residing in the underworld. The image of an underworld where the dead live in shadow is common to the Ancient Near East, in Biblical Hebrew expressed by the term tsalmaveth, literally "death-shadow". The Witch of Endor in the First Book of Samuel notably conjures the ghost (owb) of Samuel.
Salience	The salience of an item - be it an object, a person, a pixel, etc - is the state or quality by which it stands out relative to its neighbours. Saliency detection is considered to be a key attentional mechanism that facilitates learning and survival by enabling organisms to focus their limited perceptual and cognitive resources on the most pertinent subset of the available sensory data. Saliency typically arises from contrasts between items and their neighborhood, such as a red dot surrounded by white dots, a flickering message indicator of an answering machine, or a loud noise in an otherwise quiet environment.
Self-disclosure	Self-disclosure is both the conscious and unconscious act of revealing more about oneself to others. This may include, but is not limited to, thoughts, feelings, aspirations, goals, failures, successes, fears, dreams as well as one's likes, dislikes, and favorites.

Typically, a self-disclosure happens when we initially meet someone and continues as we build and develop our relationships with people. As we get to know each other, we disclose information about ourselves. If one person is not willing to "self-disclose" then the other person may stop disclosing information about themselves as well.

Introspection

Introspection is the self-observation and reporting of conscious inner thoughts, desires and sensations. It is a conscious mental and usually purposive process relying on thinking, reasoning, and examining one's own thoughts, feelings, and, in more spiritual cases, one's soul. It can also be called contemplation of one's self, and is contrasted with extrospection, the observation of things external to one's self.

Resistance

"Resistance" as initially used by Sigmund Freud, referred to patients blocking memories from conscious memory. This was a key concept, since the primary treatment method of Freud's talk therapy required making these memories available to the patient's consciousness.

"Resistance" expanded

Later, Freud described five different forms of resistance.

Assimilation

Assimilation is a common phonological process by which the phonetics of a speech segment becomes more like that of another segment in a word (or at a word boundary). A common example of assimilation would be "don't be silly" where the /n/ and /t/ in "don't" are assimilated to /m/ and /p/ by the following /b/, where said naturally in many accents and discourse styles ("dombe silly"). Assimilation can be synchronic being an active process in a language at a given point in time or diachronic being a historical sound change.

Understanding

Understanding is a psychological process related to an abstract or physical object, such as a person, situation, or message whereby one is able to think about it and use concepts to deal adequately with that object.

An understanding is the limit of a conceptualization. To understand something is to have conceptualized it to a given measure.

Internalization

Generally, internalization is the long-term process of consolidating and embedding one's own beliefs, attitudes, and values, when it comes to moral behavior. The accomplishment of this may involve the deliberate use of psychoanalytical or behavioral methods. When changing moral behavior, one is said to be "internalized" when a new set of beliefs, attitudes, and values replaces or habituates the desired behavior. For example, such internalization might take place following religious conversion.

Protestant work ethic

The Protestant work ethic is a concept in sociology, economics and history, attributable to the work of Max Weber. It is based upon the notion that the Calvinist emphasis on the necessity for hard work as a component of a person's calling and worldly success and as a sign of personal salvation.

It is argued that Protestants beginning with Martin Luther had reconceptualised worldly work as a duty which benefits both the individual and society as a whole. Thus, the Catholic idea of good works was transformed into an obligation to work diligently as a sign of grace. Whereas Catholicism teaches that good works are required of Catholics to be saved (viewing salvation as a future event), the Reformers taught that good works were only a consequence of an already-received salvation.

Competence

In American law, competence concerns the mental capacity of an individual to participate in legal proceedings. Defendants that do not possess sufficient "competence" are usually excluded from criminal prosecution, while witnesses found not to possess requisite competence cannot testify. The English equivalent is fitness to plead.

Blindness

Blindness is the condition of lacking visual perception due to physiological or neurological factors.

Various scales have been developed to describe the extent of vision loss and define blindness. Total blindness is the complete lack of form and visual light perception and is clinically recorded as NLP, an abbreviation for "no light perception." Blindness is frequently used to describe severe visual impairment with residual vision.

Capacity

The capacity of both natural and legal persons determines whether they may make binding amendments to their rights, duties and obligations, such as getting married or merging, entering into contracts, making gifts, or writing a valid will. Capacity is an aspect of status and both are defined by a person's personal law:

- for natural persons, the law of domicile or lex domicilii in common law jurisdictions, and either the law of nationality or lex patriae, or of habitual residence in civil law states;
- for legal persons, the law of the place of incorporation, the lex incorporationis for companies while other forms of business entity derive their capacity either from the law of the place in which they were formed or the laws of the states in which they establish a presence for trading purposes depending on the nature of the entity and the transactions entered into.

When the law limits or bars a person from engaging in specified activities, any agreements or contracts to do so are either voidable or void for incapacity. Sometimes such legal incapacity is referred to as incompetence.

Advocacy

Advocacy by an individual or by an advocacy group normally aim to influence public-policy and resource allocation decisions within political, economic, and social systems and institutions; it may be motivated from moral, ethical or faith principles or simply to protect an asset of interest. Advocacy can include many activities that a person or organization undertakes including media campaigns, public speaking, commissioning and publishing research or poll or the 'filing of friend of the court briefs'. Lobbying (often by Lobby groups) is a form of advocacy where a direct approach is made to legislators on an issue which plays a significant role in modern politics.

Discipline

In its most general sense, discipline refers to systematic instruction given to a disciple. it is also known as sesencd witch means seasons or tempritrue. To discipline son to follow a particular code of conduct or "order".

Selective serotonin reuptake inhibitor

Selective serotonin reuptake inhibitors or serotonin-specific reuptake inhibitor are a class of compounds typically used as antidepressants in the treatment of depression, anxiety disorders, and some personality disorders. They are also typically effective and used in treating some cases of insomnia.

Selective serotonin reuptake inhibitors are believed to increase the extracellular level of the neurotransmitter serotonin by inhibiting its reuptake into the presynaptic cell, increasing the level of serotonin in the synaptic cleft available to bind to the postsynaptic receptor.

Reuptake

Reuptake is the reabsorption of a neurotransmitter by a neurotransmitter transporter of a pre-synaptic neuron after it has performed its function of transmitting a neural impulse.

Reuptake is necessary for normal synaptic physiology because it allows for the recycling of neurotransmitters and regulates the level of neurotransmitter present in the synapse and controls how long a signal resulting from neurotransmitter release lasts. Because neurotransmitters are too large and hydrophilic to diffuse through the membrane, specific transport proteins are necessary for the reabsorption of neurotransmitters. Much research, both biochemical and structural, has been performed to obtain clues about the mechanism of reuptake.

Serotonin

Serotonin is a monoamine neurotransmitter. Biochemically derived from tryptophan, serotonin is primarily found in the gastrointestinal (GI) tract, platelets, and in the central nervous system (CNS) of animals including humans. It is a well-known contributor to feelings of well-being; therefore it is also known as a "happiness hormone" despite not being a hormone.

Color blindness

Color blindness is the decreased ability to perceive differences between some of the colors that others can distinguish. It is most often of genetic nature, but may also occur because of some eye, nerve, or brain damage, or exposure to certain chemicals. The English chemist John Dalton published the first scientific paper on this subject in 1798, "Extraordinary facts relating to the vision of colours", after the realization of his own color blindness. Because of Dalton's work, the condition was often called daltonism, although this term is now used for a type of color blindness called deuteranopia.

Alcoholism

Alcoholism is a disabling addictive disorder. It is characterized by compulsive and uncontrolled consumption of alcohol despite its negative effects on the drinker's health, relationships, and social standing. Like other drug addictions, alcoholism is medically defined as a treatable disease.

Mood disorder

Mood disorder is the term designating a group of diagnoses in the Diagnostic and Statistical Manual of Mental Disorders (DSM IV TR) classification system where a disturbance in the person's mood is hypothesized to be the main underlying feature. The classification is known as mood (affective) disorders in ICD 10.

Acculturation	Acculturation is the exchange of cultural features that results when groups of individuals having different cultures come into continuous first hand contact; the original cultural patterns of either or both groups may be altered, but the groups remain distinct. Despite definitions and evidence that acculturation entails two-way processes of change, research and theory have continued with a focus on the adjustments and changes experienced by minorities in response to their contact with the dominant majority. Thus, acculturation can be conceived to be the processes of cultural learning imposed upon minorities by the fact of being minorities.
Domestic violence	Domestic violence can be broadly defined as a pattern of abusive behaviors by one or both partners in an intimate relationship such as marriage, dating, family, friends or cohabitation. Domestic violence has many forms including physical aggression (hitting, kicking, biting, shoving, restraining, slapping, throwing objects), or threats thereof; sexual abuse; emotional abuse; controlling or domineering; intimidation; stalking; passive/covert abuse (e.g., neglect); and economic deprivation. Alcohol consumption and mental illness can be co-morbid with abuse, and present additional challenges when present alongside patterns of abuse.
Suicide	Suicide is the act of a human being intentionally causing his or her own death. Suicide is often committed out of despair, or attributed to some underlying mental disorder which includes depression, bipolar disorder, schizophrenia, alcoholism and drug abuse. Financial difficulties, troubles with interpersonal relationships and other undesirable situations play a significant role.
Feminization	Feminization is used to describe the practice, especially in female dominance, of switching the gender role of a male submissive. It is usually achieved through cross-dressing, where the male is dressed in female attire, ranging from just wearing female undergarments to being fully dressed in very feminine attire and make-up. Some males take on tasks, behaviours and roles that are overtly feminine, and adopt female mannerisms and postures in task such as sitting, walking and acting in a feminine manner.
Fetal alcohol syndrome	Fetal/Foetal alcohol syndrome is a pattern of mental and physical defects that can develop in a fetus when a woman drinks alcohol during pregnancy. The timing and frequency of alcohol consumption during pregnancy are major factors in the risk of a child developing fetal alcohol syndrome. While the ingestion of alcohol does not always result in Fetal alcohol syndrome, there are no medically established guidelines for safe levels of alcohol consumption during pregnancy.

Substance abuse	Substance abuse refers to a maladaptive pattern of use of a substance that is not considered dependent. The term "drug abuse" does not exclude dependency, but is otherwise used in a similar manner in nonmedical contexts. The terms have a huge range of definitions related to taking a psychoactive drug or performance enhancing drug for a non-therapeutic or non-medical effect.
Knowledge	Knowledge is defined by the Oxford English Dictionary as (i) expertise, and skills acquired by a person through experience or education; the theoretical or practical understanding of a subject; (ii) what is known in a particular field or in total; facts and information; or (iii) be absolutely certain or sure about something. Philosophical debates in general start with Plato's formulation of knowledge as "justified true belief." There is however no single agreed definition of knowledge presently, nor any prospect of one, and there remain numerous competing theories. Knowledge acquisition involves complex cognitive processes: perception, learning, communication, association and reasoning.
Psychotherapy	Psychotherapy is an intentional interpersonal relationship used by trained psychotherapists to aid a client or patient in problems of living. It is a talking therapy and aims to increase the individual's sense of their own well-being. Psychotherapists employ a range of techniques based on experiential relationship building, dialogue, communication and behavior change that are designed to improve the mental health of a client or patient, or to improve group relationships (such as in a family).
Intervention	An intervention is an orchestrated attempt by one, or often many, people (usually family and friends) to get someone to seek professional help with an addiction or some kind of traumatic event or crisis, or other serious problem. The term intervention is most often used when the traumatic event involves addiction to drugs or other items. Intervention can also refer to the act of using a technique within a therapy session.
Family therapy	Family therapy, also referred to as couple and family therapy and family systems therapy, is a branch of psychotherapy that works with families and couples in intimate relationships to nurture change and development. It tends to view change in terms of the systems of interaction between family members. It emphasizes family relationships as an important factor in psychological health.

Machismo	Machismo is prominently exhibited or excessive masculinity. As an attitude, machismo ranges from a personal sense of virility to a more extreme male chauvinism.
Spirituality	Spirituality can refer to an ultimate or immaterial reality; an inner path enabling a person to discover the essence of their being; or the "deepest values and meanings by which people live." Spiritual practices, including meditation, prayer and contemplation, are intended to develop an individual's inner life; such practices often lead to an experience of connectedness with a larger reality, yielding a more comprehensive self; with other individuals or the human community; with nature or the cosmos; or with the divine realm. Spirituality is often experienced as a source of inspiration or orientation in life. It can encompass belief in immaterial realities or experiences of the immanent or transcendent nature of the world.
Acculturation	Acculturation is the exchange of cultural features that results when groups of individuals having different cultures come into continuous first hand contact; the original cultural patterns of either or both groups may be altered, but the groups remain distinct. Despite definitions and evidence that acculturation entails two-way processes of change, research and theory have continued with a focus on the adjustments and changes experienced by minorities in response to their contact with the dominant majority. Thus, acculturation can be conceived to be the processes of cultural learning imposed upon minorities by the fact of being minorities.
Diagnostic and Statistical Manual of Mental Disorders	The Diagnostic and Statistical Manual of Mental Disorders is published by the American Psychiatric Association and provides a common language and standard criteria for the classification of mental disorders. It is used in the South States and in varying degrees around the world, by clinicians, researchers, psychiatric drug regulation agencies, health insurance companies, pharmaceutical companies, and policy makers.
Mental Disorder	A mental disorder is a psychological or behavioral pattern generally associated with subjective distress or disability that occurs in an individual, and which is not a part of normal development or culture. The recognition and understanding of mental health conditions has changed over time and across cultures, and there are still variations in the definition, assessment, and classification of mental disorders, although standard guideline criteria are widely accepted. A few mental disorders are diagnosed based on the harm to others, regardless of the subject's perception of distress.

Multiracial	The terms multiracial and mixed-race describe people whose ancestries come from multiple races. Unlike the term biracial, which often is only used to refer to having parents or grandparents of two different races, the term multiracial may encompass biracial people but can also include people with more than two races in their heritage, or also may refer to the origin of more generationally distant genetic admixtures of more than one race in a person's DNA.
Hate crime	Hate crimes (also known as bias-motivated crimes) occur when a perpetrator targets a victim because of his or her perceived membership in a certain social group, usually defined by racial group, religion, sexual orientation, disability, class, ethnicity, nationality, age, gender, gender identity, social status or political affiliation. Hate crime generally refers to criminal acts that are seen to have been motivated by bias against one or more of the types above, or of their derivatives. Incidents may involve physical assault, damage to property, bullying, harassment, verbal abuse or insults, or offensive graffiti or letters (hate mail).
Islam	Islam is the monotheistic religion articulated by the Qur'an, a text considered by its adherents to be the verbatim word of God, and by the teachings and normative example (called the Sunnah and Hadith) of Muhammad, considered as the last Prophet of Islam. The word Islam means 'submission to God', and an adherent of Islam is called a Muslim.
Naveed Afzal Haq	Naveed Afzal Haq is a convicted murderer who was convicted for the July 2006 Seattle Jewish Federation shooting. Murder and hate crime conviction Haq, who went on a deadly shooting spree inside the Jewish Federation of Greater Seattle facility, was found guilty of murder and a hate crime.

Naveed Haq was convicted Tuesday, December 15, 2009, of aggravated murder, malicious harassment--Washington's hate-crime statute--five counts of attempted first-degree murder and one count of unlawful imprisonment, The Seattle Times reported Wednesday, December 16, 2009. The jury did not accept the defense argument that Haq was criminally insane when the shootings occurred July 28, 2006.

Ku Klux Klan

Ku Klux Klan is the name of three distinct past and present far-right organizations in the United States, which have advocated extremist reactionary currents such as white supremacy, white nationalism, and anti-immigration, historically expressed through terrorism. Since the mid-20th century, the Ku Klux Klan has also been anti-communist. The current manifestation is splintered into several chapters and is classified as a hate group.

Intervention

An intervention is an orchestrated attempt by one, or often many, people (usually family and friends) to get someone to seek professional help with an addiction or some kind of traumatic event or crisis, or other serious problem. The term intervention is most often used when the traumatic event involves addiction to drugs or other items. Intervention can also refer to the act of using a technique within a therapy session.

Posttraumatic Stress Disorder

Posttraumatic stress disorder is a severe anxiety disorder that can develop after exposure to any event that results in psychological trauma. This event may involve the threat of death to oneself or to someone else, or to one's own or someone else's physical, sexual, or psychological integrity, overwhelming the individual's ability to cope. As an effect of psychological trauma, PTSD is less frequent and more enduring than the more commonly seen acute stress response.

Body language

Body language is a form of non-verbal communication, which consists of body posture, gestures, facial expressions, and eye movements. Humans send and interpret such signals subconsciously.

John Borg attests that human communication consists of 93 percent body language and paralinguistic cues, while only 7% of communication consists of words themselves; however, Albert Mehrabian, the researcher whose 1960s work is the source of these statistics, has stated that this is a misunderstanding of the findings.

Dissociation	Dissociation is a partial or complete disruption of the normal integration of a person's conscious or psychological functioning. Dissociation can be a response to trauma or drugs and perhaps allows the mind to distance itself from experiences that are too much for the psyche to process at that time. Dissociative disruptions can affect any aspect of a person's functioning.
Domestic violence	Domestic violence can be broadly defined as a pattern of abusive behaviors by one or both partners in an intimate relationship such as marriage, dating, family, friends or cohabitation. Domestic violence has many forms including physical aggression (hitting, kicking, biting, shoving, restraining, slapping, throwing objects), or threats thereof; sexual abuse; emotional abuse; controlling or domineering; intimidation; stalking; passive/covert abuse (e.g., neglect); and economic deprivation. Alcohol consumption and mental illness can be co-morbid with abuse, and present additional challenges when present alongside patterns of abuse.
Microaggression	Microaggression is a theory of specific interaction between those of different cultures which focuses on interactions experienced as non-physical aggression. It involves demeaning implications and other subtle insults. Microaggressions have been defined as, "brief and commonplace daily verbal, behavioral, or environmental indignities, whether intentional or unintentional, that communicate hostile, derogatory, or negative racial slights and insults toward people of color." The term "microaggression" was originally coined by Chester M. Pierce in the 1970s in terms of racial microaggression: "The chief vehicle for proracist behaviors are microaggressions. These are subtle, stunning, often automatic, and non-verbal exchanges which are 'put-downs' of blacks by offenders".
Anxiety	Anxiety is a psychological and physiological state characterized by somatic, emotional, cognitive, and behavioral components. The root meaning of the word anxiety is 'to vex or trouble'; in either the absence or presence of psychological stress, anxiety can create feelings of fear, worry, uneasiness and dread. Anxiety is considered to be a normal reaction to stress.
Anxiety Disorder	Anxiety disorders are blanket terms covering several different forms of abnormal and pathological fear and anxiety which only came under the aegis of psychiatry at the very end of the 19th century. Gelder, Mayou ' Geddes (2005) explains that anxiety disorders are classified in two groups: continuous symptoms and episodic symptoms. Current psychiatric diagnostic criteria recognize a wide variety of anxiety disorders.
Depression	Depression is a state of low mood and aversion to activity that can affect a person's thoughts, behaviour, feelings and physical well-being. It may include feelings of sadness, anxiety, emptiness, hopelessness, worthlessness, guilt, irritability, or restlessness. Depressed people may lose interest in activities that once were pleasurable, experience difficulty concentrating, remembering details, or making decisions, and may contemplate or attempt suicide.

Generalized Anxiety Disorder	Generalized anxiety disorder is an anxiety disorder that is characterized by excessive, uncontrollable and often irrational worry about everyday things that is disproportionate to the actual source of worry. This excessive worry often interferes with daily functioning, as individuals suffering Generalized anxiety disorder typically anticipate disaster, and are overly concerned about everyday matters such as health issues, money, death, family problems, friend problems, relationship problems or work difficulties. They often exhibit a variety of physical symptoms, including fatigue, fidgeting, headaches, nausea, numbness in hands and feet, muscle tension, muscle aches, difficulty swallowing, bouts of difficulty breathing, difficulty concentrating, trembling, twitching, irritability, agitation, sweating, restlessness, insomnia, hot flashes, and rashes and inability to fully control the anxiety.
Perception	In philosophy, psychology, and cognitive science, perception is the process of attaining awareness or understanding of sensory information. The word "perception" comes from the Latin words perceptio, percipio, and means "receiving, collecting, action of taking possession, apprehension with the mind or senses." Perception is one of the oldest fields in psychology. The oldest quantitative law in psychology is the Weber-Fechner law, which quantifies the relationship between the intensity of physical stimuli and their perceptual effects (for example, testing how much darker a computer screen can get before the viewer actually notices).
Coming out	Coming out (of the closet) is a figure of speech for lesbian, gay, bisexual, and transgender (LGBT) and Asexual people's disclosure of their sexual orientation and/or gender identity. Framed and debated as a privacy issue, coming out of the closet is described and experienced variously as: a psychological process or journey; decision-making or risk-taking; a strategy or plan; a mass or public event; a speech act and a matter of personal identity; a rite of passage; liberation or emancipation from oppression; a means toward feeling gay pride instead of shame and social stigma; or even career suicide. Author Steven Seidman writes that "it is the power of the closet to shape the core of an individual's life that has made homosexuality into a significant personal, social, and political drama in twentieth-century America."

Mental health	Mental health describes either a level of cognitive or emotional well-being or an absence of a mental disorder. From perspectives of the discipline of positive psychology or holism mental health may include an individual's ability to enjoy life and procure a balance between life activities and efforts to achieve psychological resilience. Mental health is an expression of our emotions and signifies a successful adaptation to a range of demands.
Alcoholism	Alcoholism is a disabling addictive disorder. It is characterized by compulsive and uncontrolled consumption of alcohol despite its negative effects on the drinker's health, relationships, and social standing. Like other drug addictions, alcoholism is medically defined as a treatable disease.
Substance abuse	Substance abuse refers to a maladaptive pattern of use of a substance that is not considered dependent. The term "drug abuse" does not exclude dependency, but is otherwise used in a similar manner in nonmedical contexts. The terms have a huge range of definitions related to taking a psychoactive drug or performance enhancing drug for a non-therapeutic or non-medical effect.
Suicide	Suicide is the act of a human being intentionally causing his or her own death. Suicide is often committed out of despair, or attributed to some underlying mental disorder which includes depression, bipolar disorder, schizophrenia, alcoholism and drug abuse. Financial difficulties, troubles with interpersonal relationships and other undesirable situations play a significant role.
Selective serotonin reuptake inhibitor	Selective serotonin reuptake inhibitors or serotonin-specific reuptake inhibitor are a class of compounds typically used as antidepressants in the treatment of depression, anxiety disorders, and some personality disorders. They are also typically effective and used in treating some cases of insomnia. Selective serotonin reuptake inhibitors are believed to increase the extracellular level of the neurotransmitter serotonin by inhibiting its reuptake into the presynaptic cell, increasing the level of serotonin in the synaptic cleft available to bind to the postsynaptic receptor.
Reuptake	Reuptake is the reabsorption of a neurotransmitter by a neurotransmitter transporter of a pre-synaptic neuron after it has performed its function of transmitting a neural impulse.

	Reuptake is necessary for normal synaptic physiology because it allows for the recycling of neurotransmitters and regulates the level of neurotransmitter present in the synapse and controls how long a signal resulting from neurotransmitter release lasts. Because neurotransmitters are too large and hydrophilic to diffuse through the membrane, specific transport proteins are necessary for the reabsorption of neurotransmitters. Much research, both biochemical and structural, has been performed to obtain clues about the mechanism of reuptake.
Serotonin	Serotonin is a monoamine neurotransmitter. Biochemically derived from tryptophan, serotonin is primarily found in the gastrointestinal (GI) tract, platelets, and in the central nervous system (CNS) of animals including humans. It is a well-known contributor to feelings of well-being; therefore it is also known as a "happiness hormone" despite not being a hormone.
Love	Love is a universal concept related to affinity, with different interpretations depending on the point of view taken (personal, philosophic, artistic, religious, scientific). In the Western World, love is considered an emotion of strong affection and personal attachment. In philosophical context, love is a virtue representing all of human kindness, compassion, and affection.

CPSIA information can be obtained at www.ICGtesting.com
Printed in the USA
BVOW030715240512

290891BV00001B/10/P

9 781617 448614